Dedication

This book is dedicated to my daughters Jessica and Chloe who continue to amaze me every day with their strong will and determination to overcome anything life throws their way and their unfaltering belief that good will always prevail!

Silly Circus ABCs

Deborah Jaeger
Copyright © 2017

ISBN-13 978-0692958209
ISBN-10 0692958207

A

Amazing aerial acrobats are flying through the air!

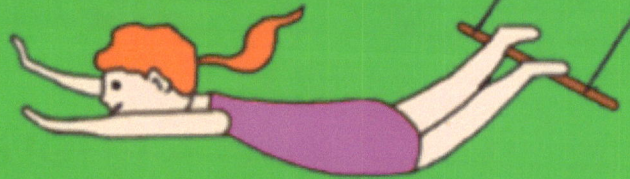

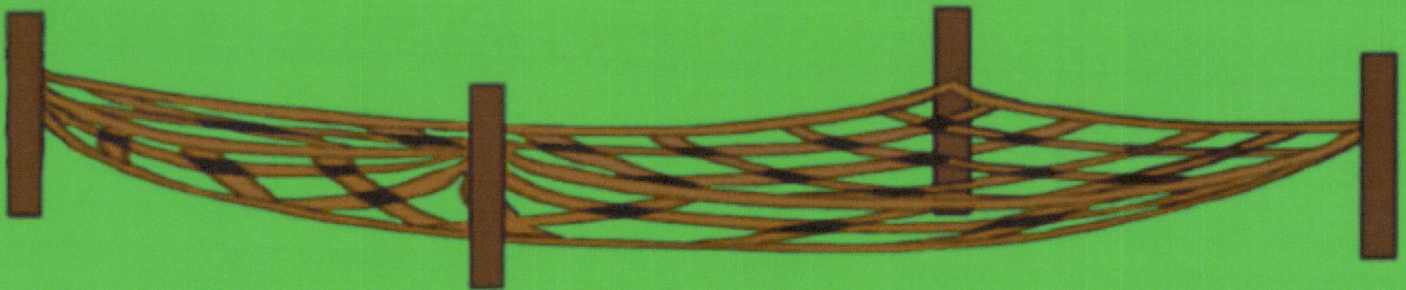

B Blue balloons and bright beach balls are bouncing everywhere!

C Chaotic clowns with caps and canes are causing quite a tizzy!

D Dogs in dresses dance around making themselves dizzy!

E

Eight enormous elephants are balancing on eggs!

F Frolicking foxes
are hopping fences
with stilts on all four legs!

G A gymnast standing on his hands spitting green gummy fishes!

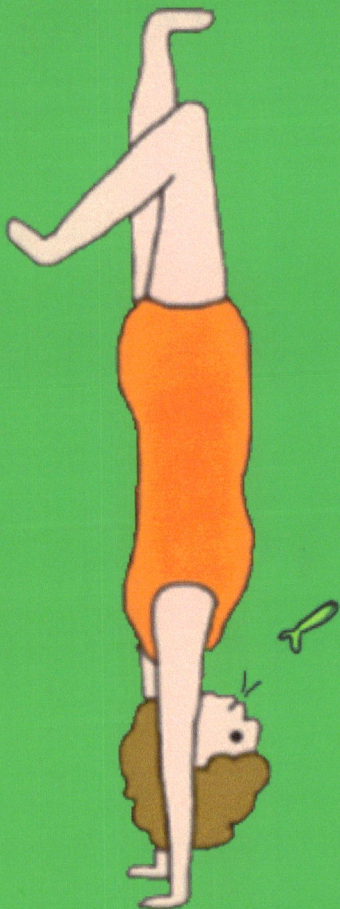

H

Happy hippos in hammocks,
holding sticks,
spinning dishes!

I

An iguana with an icebox selling icecream cones and pop!

POP
50¢

ICECREAM CONES
$ 1.00

J

A juggler
juggling
jars of
jam
while
standing
on a top!

K A kangaroo in a kayak playing a kazoo!

L

Lazy lions show up late
in a limo painted blue!

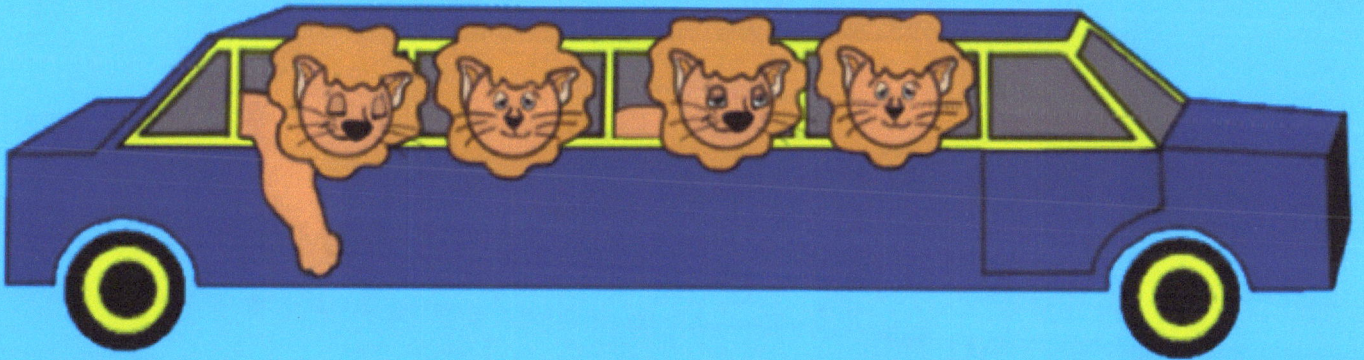

M

Musical mice with mo-hawks are marching in a band!

N

Nudging narwhals
wait to jump,
into a net they'll land!

O An octopus with oars
is swatting oranges into jars!

P Penguins wearing pajamas are driving fast in purple cars!

Q

Quail watch quietly
from their quilted nest.

R The ringmaster runs the show wearing his ritzy vest!

S

A silly slippery seal
is balancing a beach ball
on it's snout!

T

A trainer with a top hat and tigers acting out!

U

A cowboy riding a **u**nicorn while holding an **u**mbrella!

V Viking vultures in a van are singing acapella!

W

Wobbly walrus with whiskers are blowing bubbles with their gum!

An o**x** is standing on a bo**x** beating on a drum!

Y

The yellow yak is yawning
Its been a long... long day.

Z The zany zebra trots around with stripes of pink and gray!

....THE END

www.ingramcontent.com/pod-product-compliance
Lightning Source LLC
Chambersburg PA
CBHW042107040426
42448CB00002B/172